SCIENTISTS AT WORK

ANDERS
CELSIUS

FERNANDO GORDON

Consulting Editor, Diane Craig, M.A./Reading Specialist

Super Sandcastle

An Imprint of Abdo Publishing
abdopublishing.com

abdopublishing.com

Published by Abdo Publishing, a division of ABDO, PO Box 398166, Minneapolis, Minnesota 55439. Copyright © 2017 by Abdo Consulting Group, Inc. International copyrights reserved in all countries. No part of this book may be reproduced in any form without written permission from the publisher. Super SandCastle™ is a trademark and logo of Abdo Publishing.

Printed in the United States of America, North Mankato, Minnesota
062016
092016

THIS BOOK CONTAINS
RECYCLED MATERIALS

Editor: Rebecca Felix
Content Developer: Nancy Tuminelly
Cover and Interior Design and Production: Mighty Media, Inc.
Photo Credits: Courtesy of the Smithsonian Libraries, Washington, DC; Mighty Media, Inc.; Public Domain; Science Source; Shutterstock; SSPL/Getty Images; Wikimedia Commons

Library of Congress Cataloging-in-Publication Data
Names: Gordon, Fernando, author.
Title: Anders Celsius / by Fernando Gordon ; consulting editor, Diane Craig,
    M.A./reading specialist.
Description: Minneapolis, Minnesota : Abdo Publishing, [2017] | Series:
    Scientists at work
Identifiers: LCCN 2016001426 (print) | LCCN 2016007321 (ebook) | ISBN
    9781680781533 (print) | ISBN 9781680775969 (ebook)
Subjects: LCSH: Celsius, Anders, 1701-1744--Juvenile literature. |
    Physicists--Sweden--Biography--Juvenile literature. | Astronomers
    --Sweden--Biography--Juvenile literature. | Temperature measurements
    --History--Juvenile literature. | Sweden--Biography--Juvenile literature.
Classification: LCC QC16.C38 G67 2017 (print) | LCC QC16.C38 (ebook) | DDC
    530.092--dc23
LC record available at http://lccn.loc.gov/2016001426

Super SandCastle™ books are created by a team of professional educators, reading specialists, and content developers around five essential components—phonemic awareness, phonics, vocabulary, text comprehension, and fluency—to assist young readers as they develop reading skills and strategies and increase their general knowledge. All books are written, reviewed, and leveled for guided reading, early reading intervention, and Accelerated Reader™ programs for use in shared, guided, and independent reading and writing activities to support a balanced approach to literacy instruction.

CONTENTS

ANDERS CELSIUS

Anders Celsius was a scientist. He is known for the Celsius **temperature** scale. He also studied the stars.

Some stars are brighter than others. Celsius found a way to measure a star's brightness.

ANDERS CELSIUS

BORN: November 27, 1701, Uppsala, Sweden

MARRIED: never married

CHILDREN: none

DIED: April 25, 1744, Uppsala, Sweden

A SCIENTIFIC FAMILY TREE

Anders grew up in Uppsala, Sweden. He learned science and math at an early age. His father was a scientist. So was one grandfather.

Uppsala is on the Fyris River.

His other grandfather was a **mathematician**. Anders followed in the footsteps of both grandfathers.

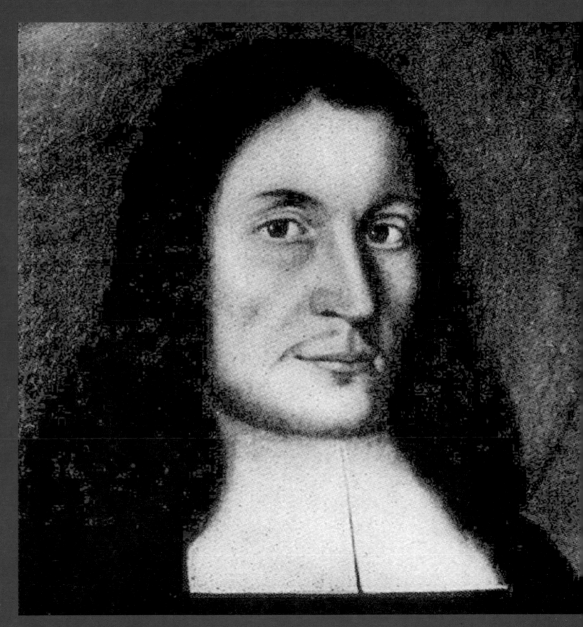

Celsius's grandfather, Magnus Celsius

PROFESSOR CELSIUS

Celsius studied at Uppsala University. He became a **professor** in 1730. He was only 29 years old! He taught **astronomy**.

Uppsala University is the oldest university in Sweden. It was founded in 1477.

Today's astronomers use much better telescopes than Celsius had.

AURORA BOREALIS

Aurora borealis is a natural light display. It appears in the sky. It happens near the North Pole. It is also called "northern lights."

NORTH POLE

SWEDEN

Celsius studied aurora borealis for years. He made new discoveries about what causes it.

CELSIUS'S TRAVELS

In 1732, Celsius left Uppsala. He went to other countries. He visited **observatories**. Celsius met with famous **astronomers**.

Celsius met astronomer Christfried Kirch in Berlin, Germany.

One of the cities Celsius went to was Nuremberg, Germany.

It was known as a center for **astronomy**.

THE LAPLAND EXPEDITION

In 1736, Celsius began another adventure. He went to Lapland. It is near the North Pole. A French **astronomer** led the **expedition**. His name was Pierre-Louis Moreau de Maupertuis. They measured the curve of the Earth.

Pierre-Louis Moreau de Maupertuis

Other scientists went to the **equator**. They made the same measurement there.

The measurements didn't match. This proved that Earth isn't perfectly round! Earth is slightly flat at the poles.

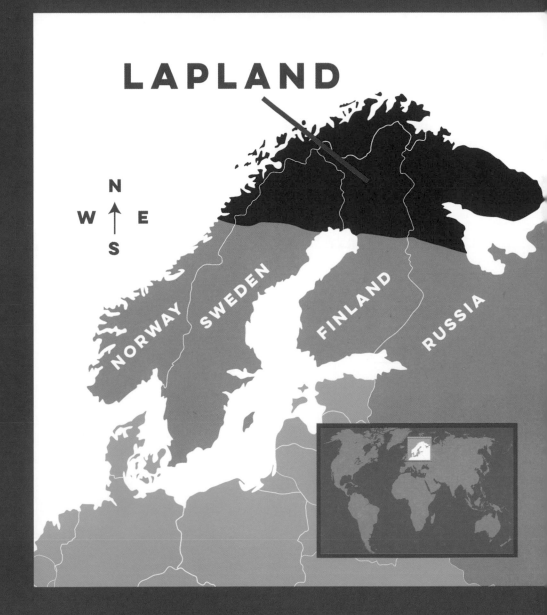

LAPLAND

N
W ← → E
S

NORWAY

SWEDEN

FINLAND

RUSSIA

THE CELSIUS OBSERVATORY

The Lapland **expedition** made Celsius famous. This helped him raise money. He used the money to build an **observatory**. It opened in 1741. It is in Uppsala.

Anders Celsius

ASTRONOMISKA OBSERVATORIUM

The Uppsala Astronomical Observatory. Celsius lived in the building too.

MEASURING TEMPERATURE

Celsius invented a **temperature** scale. Scientists measured temperature in different ways. Celsius wanted one standard system.

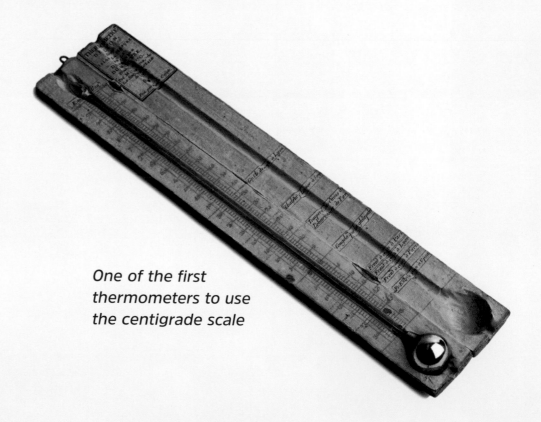

One of the first thermometers to use the centigrade scale

Celsius created a scale in 1742. He called it the centigrade scale. His system caught on quickly. It is still used today.

Many thermometers today show two scales. One is the Fahrenheit scale. The other is the centigrade, or Celsius, scale.

ADVANCING SCIENCE

Celsius's **temperature** scale helped standardize scientific **research**. Scientists used the same system. This meant they could compare their results.

Thermometers are often used in science experiments.

Anders Celsius

MORE ABOUT CELSIUS

The CENTIGRADE SCALE was renamed Celsius in his honor.

Celsius measured the brightness of 300 different STARS.

Celsius died of a disease that affects the LUNGS. He was only 42.

TEST YOUR KNOWLEDGE

1. Celsius's father was a **mathematician**. *True or false?*

2. How old was Celsius when he became a **professor**?

3. Where did Celsius go in 1736?

THINK ABOUT IT!

What is the coolest thing you've seen in the night sky?

GLOSSARY

astronomy – the study of objects and matter outside Earth's atmosphere. Someone who studies astronomy is an astronomer.

equator – an imaginary circle around the middle of Earth. It is halfway between the North and South poles.

expedition – a trip taken for a specific purpose.

mathematician – an expert in the study of numbers and shapes and how they work together.

observatory – a place or a building for observing the weather or outer space.

professor – someone who teaches at a college or university.

research – a study of something to learn new information.

temperature – a measure of how hot or cold something is.